SPELLING

RULES and PRACTICE 3

Susan J. Daughtrey M.Ed.

Childs World Education Limited
1995

C O N T E N T S

e AT THE END OF A WORD

At the end of a word, *e* says nothing at all but has several important jobs to do.

1. *e* placed at the end of a word makes a vowel say its *name*.

A vowel will be *short*, and so say its *sound*, unless there is a reason for it to be *long*. To create a *long* vowel which says its *name*, another vowel usually needs to be nearby. This can be either next to it, as in a *vowel digraph*, or with only one consonant between two vowels.

There are three things we can do to make a vowel *long*:

A. Place a *silent e* on the end of the word which follows the pattern:
> vowel - consonant - *silent e*

Example:

pin + e	=	pine
ton + e	=	tone
cut + e	=	cute

B. Place two vowels together and so create a *vowel digraph* which makes one vowel sound:

Example:

ai makes a	long *a* sound	tr*ai*n
ee makes a	long *e* sound	m*ee*t
ie makes a	long *i* sound	t*ie*
oa makes a	long *o* sound	s*oa*p
ue makes a	long *u* sound	c*ue*

(We looked at the function of a *silent e* and *vowel digraphs* in Book One of this Series.)

C. At the end of an *open syllable*.

The only other reason for a vowel to be *long* and so say its *name* is the position of the vowel in the syllable when the word is broken up into syllables. Every syllable has one vowel sound. An *open syllable* ends in a vowel and the vowel sound is *long*. A *closed syllable* ends in a consonant, and the vowel sound is *short*.

Example:

OPEN		CLOSED
sta' tion	compare	stag' nant
hu' man	compare	hun' ter
vo' cal	compare	vol' cano

(*Syllables* were studied in detail in Book Two of this Series.)

There are FOUR other jobs an *e* at the end of a word can do:

2. An English word never ends in *v*. At the end of a word an *e* always follows a *v*.

Example:

love

give

have

In these three cases the *e* is not a *silent e* but is simply being used to 'stick on' the *v*.

Example:

stove

trove

hive

In these cases the *e* at the end of the word has two functions:

a. To make the vowel *long*.(A *silent e*.)

b. To 'stick on' the *v*.

3. To make a *soft c* sound. To make c say s.

Example:

chance

romance

notice

In all these cases the *e* at the end of the word is simply changing the sound of the *c* to say *s*.

Example:

grace

place

mice

Here again the *e* has two jobs to do:

a. To make the vowel *long*.(A *silent e*.)

b. To make the *c* say *s*.

4. To make a *soft g* sound. To make g say *j*.

Example:

college

hinge

knowledge

Here the *e* is simply making the *g* say *j*.

Example:

courage

stage

huge

In these cases the *e* has two jobs to do:

a. To make the vowel *long*. (A *silent e*.)

b. To make the *g* say *j*.

5. To stick *s* on to the end of a word.

If a single *s* cannot be taken off the end of a word to leave a complete, whole and sensible word, then the *s* is permanently 'stuck on' with an *e*.

Example:

house

worse

cruise

In all these cases, the *s* cannot be removed and a sensible word remain.

house	hou	not a sensible word
worse	wor	not a sensible word

Hou and *wor* - neither of these words is sensible. The *s*, therefore, must be permanently attached to the word and is 'stuck on' with the *e*.

In this respect the words below differ.

Example:

lamps

hits

calls

In all these cases, the *s* can be removed and a sensible word remain. These words are either plurals or verbs (doing words) in the third person singular (*he, she or it* hits, calls). The *s*, therefore, does not want to be permanently 'stuck on' and no *e* is necessary.

It may be possible also that the *e* that 'sticks on' the *s* is also making a vowel say its *name*:

Example:

base

case

Here the *e* is doing two jobs:

a. To make the vowel *long*. (A *silent e*.)

b. To 'stick on' the *s*.

PRACTICE : *e* AT THE END OF A WORD

An *e* at the end of a word says nothing at all but has five important jobs to do:

1. **To make a vowel say its *name*.**
2. **To follow *v* because an English word never ends in *v*.**
3. **To make *c* say *s*.**
4. **To make *g* say *j*.**
5. **To 'stick on' an *s* if you cannot take it off and be left with a sensible word.**

Exercise One: _____

The following words all end in *e*. There are five jobs an *e* can do. Using the Rules as they are listed above, write 1, 2, 3, 4 or 5 alongside each word according to the job the *e* is doing. In some cases the *e* may be doing more than one job. Then study the letter patterns, and when you are ready, copy each word onto the line provided.

house	___ _____	scarce	___ _____	suppose	___ _____
Greece	___ _____	substance	___ _____	commence	___ _____
have	___ _____	experience	___ _____	scheme	___ _____
distance	___ _____	aggressive	___ _____	noose	___ _____
delicate	___ _____	niece	___ _____	impatience	___ _____
carriage	___ _____	passage	___ _____	intelligence	___ _____
cause	___ _____	practice	___ _____	presence	___ _____
resistance	___ _____	disclose	___ _____	challenge	___ _____
positive	___ _____	believe	___ _____	grudge	___ _____
sleeve	___ _____	divide	___ _____	machine	___ _____
notice	___ _____	grease	___ _____	refuge	___ _____
receive	___ _____	accuse	___ _____	bandage	___ _____
extreme	___ _____	incline	___ _____	disguise	___ _____
negative	___ _____	discourage	___ _____	survive	___ _____
science	___ _____	enterprise	___ _____	deceive	___ _____
intimate	___ _____	revolve	___ _____	grieve	___ _____
advertise	___ _____	hedge	___ _____	turnstile	___ _____
acquire	___ _____	village	___ _____	siege	___ _____
juice	___ _____	prince	___ _____	confuse	___ _____
baggage	___ _____	slate	___ _____	misfortune	___ _____

Exercise Two: _____

Tick those words below which can have the *s* taken off and be left with a sensible word; add *e* to those words which cannot. Copy each word carefully onto the line provided.

√	√	√
hors____ __ _____	walks__ __ _____	caus____ __ _____
pianos__ __ _____	curs____ __ _____	suppos__ __ _____
els____ __ _____	lives____ __ _____	thinks__ __ _____
hous__ __ _____	cliffs__ __ _____	wors____ __ _____
nurs__ __ _____	dos____ __ _____	chas____ __ _____
thinks__ __ _____	hits__ __ _____	clos____ __ _____
goos__ __ _____	choos__ __ _____	cas____ __ _____

THE *v* RULES

There are three Rules concerning a *v* spelling:

1. Never end a word in *v* alone, always end *ve*.
Example:

> forgive
> valve
> nerve
> sleeve
> have

2. Never use *vv*, it could easily be mistaken for *w*. Only ever use a single *v*.
Example:

> discover
> diver

3. Never use *uv*. *O* before *v* says *u* so use *ov* to say *uv*.
Example:

> love
> shovel
> discover
> oven
> cover

PRACTICE : THE *v* RULES

There are three Rules concerning the *v* spelling:

1. **Never end a word in *v* alone, always end *ve*.**
2. **Never use *vv*. Only ever use a single *v*.**
3. **Never use *uv*. *O* before *v* says *u* so use *ov* to say *uv*.**

Exercise Three: _____

With reference to the above three Rules concerning the *v* spelling, correct these spellings and rewrite them.

recuvver	_____	abuv	_____	dicuvver	_____
nerv	_____	uven	_____	surviv	_____
luvver	_____	observ	_____	perceiv	_____
gav	_____	extravvagant	_____	detectiv	_____
vvulgar	_____	gluv	_____	luv	_____
curv	_____	deserv	_____	hovver	_____
arriv	_____	cuver	_____	heav	_____

It is worth noting here other words which are spelt with an *o* instead of *u*, but which make the sound of *u*.

1. Use *o* before *th* to say *u*.
Example:

> mother
> grandmother
> smother
> brother

2. In many words *o* before *n* or *m* says *u*.
Example:

> monkey
> front
> Monday
> London
> comfort
> something

Exercise Four: _____

The spaces in the words below say *u*. Fill in the spaces with *u* or *o* then rewrite the word on the line provided. When you are ready, cover over each word and try to write it from memory.

h___ney	_____	_____	disc___ver	_____	_____
m___nth	_____	_____	m___ther	_____	_____
f___dge	_____	_____	n___thing	_____	_____
ab___ve	_____	_____	am___ng	_____	_____
c___ver	_____	_____	sh___vel	_____	_____
b___bble	_____	_____	w___nder	_____	_____
br___ther	_____	_____	sh___tter	_____	_____
l___ve	_____	_____	fr___nt	_____	_____
___pper	_____	_____	ed___cate	_____	_____
c___me	_____	_____	gl___ve	_____	_____
M___nday	_____	_____	L___nd___n	_____	_____
j___stice	_____	_____	p___rple	_____	_____
an___ther	_____	_____	m___scle	_____	_____
m___nkey	_____	_____	c___mfort	_____	_____
sm___ther	_____	_____	butterc___p	_____	_____

s AT THE END OF A WORD

There are four ways of creating a hissing sound at the end of a word: *s*, *ss*, *se* and *ce*.

1. A single *s* is used at the end of a word if it possible to take it off and be left with a complete and sensible word.
Example:

cars	car
pins	pin
calls	call

In all these cases the word ending *s* is a plural noun or a verb in the third person singular.

2. **ss is used at the end of a one syllable word which has one short vowel sound. This is in accordance with the *123 Rule* which states that beginning to count at the *short* vowel, there must be three letters to the end of the word. (See Book One in this Series .)**

Example:

123

dress

cross

Exceptions to this Rule include: as   has   gas   yes   is   his   this   us   bus
These words break both Rules One and Two.

3. **When *e* follows *c*, the *c* says *s*. (See Book Two in this Series.)
At the end of a word *ce* and *se* follow a long vowel or a short vowel and a consonant.**

Example:

place

fence

prince

ce is more usual than *se* for a *hissing s* ending, so if in doubt, use *ce*. However, common *se* endings that may be worthwhile remembering include:

sparse   vase   case   chase   base   dose   loose   noose   choose

else   false   pulse   horse   course   cause   goose   geese   grease   crease

mouse   house   spouse   tense   sense   nurse   purse   curse   verse

Unlike Rule One, the *s* at the end of these words cannot be removed and a sensible word remain.
When an *s* cannot be taken off and a sensible word remain, the *s* must be permanently 'stuck on' with an *e*. This is one of the functions of an *e* at the end of a word.

PRACTICE : *s* AT THE END OF A WORD

There are four ways of creating a *hissing s* sound at the end of a word: *s*, *ss*, *se* and *ce*.

1. **Use a single *s* if you can take it off and be left with a complete word.**
2. **Use *ss* after a short vowel in accordance with the *123* Rule.**
3. **Use *ce* or *se* after a long vowel or a short vowel and a consonant.**

Ce is more usual, so when in doubt, use *ce*.

Exercise Five: _____

Read through the words ending in *se* above. Use three of them in one sentence of you own.

_____

_____

_____

Exercise Six:_____

Words ending in a *hissing s* sound.
Read and copy each of the following *hissing s* words saying aloud each letter as you do so. Study carefully the letter patterns and the syllables, and then when you are ready, cover over each word and try to write it from memory.

ss endings:

possess _____ _____   congress _____ _____

process _____ _____   confess _____ _____

impress _____ _____   digress _____ _____

suppress_____ _____   compress_____ _____

mistress_____ _____   fortress _____ _____

distress _____ _____   buttress _____ _____

success _____ _____   egress _____ _____

actress _____ _____   empress _____ _____

Using a dictionary, give the meaning of the following three words:

egress _____

empress _____

impress_____

Can you think of two more words which end in *ss*? Write them below.

_____

Exercise Seven:_____

These words end in *ce*. Study carefully the letter patterns and when you are ready copy, cover over each word, and try to write it from memory.

ce endings:

lance _____   dance _____

prance _____   farce _____

stance _____   reduce _____

produce _____   pretence _____

substance _____   sustenance _____

maintenance _____   conveyance _____

Using a dictionary, give the meaning of the following three words:

sustenance _____

maintenance_____

conveyance _____

Can you think of two more words ending in *ce*:
a. which follow a *short* vowel and a consonant? _____

b. which follow a *long* vowel sound? _____

Read through the words ending in *se* on page 8.

Exercise Eight:_____

All the following gaps say *s*. Use *s*, *ss*, *ce* or *se* to finish these words. Copy these words on the line provided, saying aloud each letter as you do so. Study the letters patterns and syllables and when you are ready, cover over each word and try to write it from memory.

congre__ _____ _____   hor___ _____ _____

pur___ _____ _____   pla___ _____ _____

sen___ _____ _____   fall___ _____ _____

thi___ _____ _____   el___ _____ _____

confe___ _____ _____   last___ _____ _____

nonsen__ _____ _____   bu___ _____ _____

prin___ _____ _____   crea___ _____ _____

lo___ _____ _____   far___ _____ _____

employ__ _____ _____   ki___ _____ _____

ga____   _____ _____   last____ _____ _____

spar____ _____ _____   fen____   _____ _____

spi____   _____ _____   bo____   _____ _____

rece____ _____ _____   empre__   _____ _____

dan____   _____ _____   sing____ _____ _____

pul____   _____ _____   mo____   _____ _____

cro____   _____ _____   redu____ _____ _____

Exercise Nine: _____

Where you need one, place an *e* on the end of any of these words. (If you cannot remove the *s* from the end of any of these words 'stick it on' with an *e*.) Then rewrite the word carefully on the line provided.

sens____   _____   knows____ _____   nonsens____ _____

calls____ _____   rins____   _____   loos____   _____

hors____   _____   greets____ _____   purs____   _____

gives____ _____   cats____   _____   falls____   _____

hous____   _____   caus____   _____   noos____   _____

els____   _____   huts____   _____   fals____   _____

picks____ _____   nurs____   _____   greas____   _____

goos____   _____   mous____   _____   seas____   _____

cars____   _____   buns____   _____   diseas____ _____

bas____   _____   sings____ _____   sees____   _____

SPELLING THE *z* SOUND

An *s* is usually pronounced *s*. Occasionally *s* has a *z* sound.

ss in the middle of a word is often pronounced *z*.
Example:

> possess
> scissors
> dissolve

Otherwise for a *z* sound:

1. Use a *z* for a *z* sound at the beginning of a word, never *s*.

Example:

> zero
> zoo
> zip
> zinc
> zoom

2. Inside a word use *zz, z, ss* or *s* for a *z* sound. *S* is most common.

Example:

> dazzle
> dizzy
> puzzle
>
> dozen
> razor
> horizon
>
> possess
> dissolve
>
> reason
> business
> cousin
> president
> transistor

3. Use *zz* only for the *z* sound at the end of a word after a short vowel sound, never *s*.

Example:

> buzz
> fizz
> fuzz
> whizz

Compare the sound of mo*ss*, lo*ss*, me*ss*, distre*ss*, stre*ss* and gla*ss* where the *ss* spelling on the end of the word gives a very definite *s* sound.

4. Use *ze* or *se* at the end of a word after a long vowel sound which follows either the pattern: vowel - consonant(*z* or *s*) - *silent e*.

Example:

> prize
> recognize *
> graze
> amuse
> these
> whose

Or, a vowel digraph:
Example:

freeze
breeze
seize
sneeze

ease
disease
please
choose
noise
because

Se is more common.

* NOTE:
recognize, organize and *realize* can be spelt with a *z* or an *s*.

PRACTICE : SPELLING THE *z* SOUND

There are four ways to spell the *z* sound:

1. **Use *z* for a *z* sound at the beginning of a word, never *s*.**
2. **Use *z*, *zz*, *s* or *ss* for a *z* sound in the middle of a word.**
3. **Use *zz* for the *z* sound at the end of a word following a *short* vowel sound, never *s*.**
4. **Use *ze* or *se* at the end of a word after a *long* vowel sound.**
   Se is more common.

Exercise Ten: _____

Each of the gaps in the following words says *z*. Fill in *s*, *ss*, *z*, *zz*, *ze* or *se* to complete each word. The words are in the Examples above to help you if necessary. Copy each word onto the line provided, saying aloud each letter as you do so. Study the letter patterns and syllables. When you are ready, cover over each word and try to write it from memory.

gra____	_____	_____	sci____ors	_____	_____
rea____on	_____	_____	fi____	_____	_____
free____	_____	_____	bree____	_____	_____
po____ess	_____	_____	becau____	_____	_____
pu____le	_____	_____	____ero	_____	_____

disea____   _____ _____   recogni___   _____ _____

amu____   _____ _____   di___y   _____ _____

____oo   _____ _____   noi___   _____ _____

da___le   _____ _____   di___olve   _____ _____

____inc   _____ _____   bu___iness   _____ _____

plea____   _____ _____   pri___   _____ _____

____oom   _____ _____   pre__ident   _____ _____

snee____   _____ _____   ____ip   _____ _____

sei____   _____ _____   choo____   _____ _____

Exercise Eleven: _____

Complete the following sentences. Each gap says *z*.

1. It was a pu____le to the student becau____ he could not understand why the ____inc did not di____olve in water.

2. As a re____ult of research, the disea____ which had affected a do____en animals at the ____oo had now been recogni____d.

3. I am plea____d my pri____ bull is allowed to gra____ without noi____ in that field.

4. Who____ cou____in and aunt will vi____it the pre____ident when the weather is rea____onable?

5. Water free____s at ____ero degrees Celcius.

6. As the sun ro____ above the hori____on, its rays da____led my eyes and made me go di____y.

7. Plea____ choo____ sci____ors with a ra____or-sharp edge becau____ they are ea____ier to cut with.

8. Amu____ yourself with the____ tran____istor radios.

FORMING THE PLURAL

We say that something is in the *SINGULAR* when we are talking about *ONE* thing (noun).

We say that something is in the *PLURAL* when we are talking about *MORE THAN ONE THING* (noun).

There are 14 Rules concerning the spelling of the plural.

1. The most usual ending is simply to add *s*.
Example:

We say	one lamp	but	two lamps
	one table		two tables
	one cat		two cats

When *s* is added to a word ending in a *soft g* or a *soft c* sound, it is sounded as a separate syllable.
Example:

	one race		two races
	one stage		two stages

2. For words which end in a hissing sound, such as *ss*, *ch*, *x*, *s* and *sh*, we add *es*. The *es* ending is sounded as a separate syllable.
Example:

We say	one church	but	two churches
	one witch		two witches
	one dress		two dresses
	one fox		two foxes

3. Words ending in a *y* which is immediately preceded by a consonant, we change the *y* to an *i* and add *es*.
Example:

We say	one baby	but	two babies
	one lady		two ladies
	one library		two libraries
	one canary		two canaries

4. However, if there is a vowel immediately in front of the *y*, we just add *s*.
Example:

We say	one monkey	but	two monkeys
	one day		two days
	one toy		two toys

5. Most words which end in *f*, we change the *f* to a *v* and add *es*.
Example:

We say	one thief	but	two thieves
	one loaf		two loaves
	one wife		two wives

These words include: elf, knife, wife, loaf, wolf, thief, shelf, life, leaf, half, calf, scarf (scarves or scarfs).

6. However, some words which end in *f* simply add *s*.

Example:

We say	one cliff	but	two cliffs
	one chief		two chiefs
	one roof		two roofs

These words include: roof, cuff, cliff, puff, chief, hoof (hoofs or hooves), belief.

7. To words ending in *o*, or a vowel plus *o*, we usually add *es*.

Example:

We say	one potato	but	two potatoes
	one tomato		two tomatoes
	one cargo		two cargoes
	one hero		two heroes

These words include: potato, tomato, volcano (volcanoes or volcanos), hero, echo.

8. However, some words ending in *o*, especially words associated with music, simply add *s*.

Example:

We say	one piano	but	two pianos
	one cello		two cellos
	one solo		two solos

These words include: piano, solo, radio, photo, cello, banjo (banjos or banjoes).

9. Some words change completely.

Example:

We say	one child	but	two children
	one tooth		two teeth
	one goose		two geese

These words include: foot/feet, man/men, tooth/teeth, goose/geese, woman/women, policeman/policemen, mouse/mice, ox/oxen.

10. Some words do not change at all.

Example:

We say	one deer	and	two deer
	one salmon		two salmon
	one sheep		two sheep

These words include: trout, cod, haddock, herring.

11. Some words are always in the plural. There is no singular form.

Example:

| We say (a pair of) | spectacles |
| | trousers |

scissors

12. Some nouns have two plural forms.
Example:

We say		
	penny	pennies or pence
	index	indices or indexes
	fish	fishes or fish

13. To nouns which are made up of more than one word (often hyphenated) add *s* to the main word.
Example:

We say			
	one brother-in-law	but	two brothers-in-law
	one passer-by		two passers-by
	one teaspoonful		two teaspoonsful

14. Words inherited from foreign languages change according to the following Rules:

Words ending in *us* change to *i*.
Example:

We say			
	one radius	but	two radii
	one fungus		two fungi
	one terminus		two termini

Words ending in *is* change to *es*.
Example:

We say			
	one thesis	but	two theses
	one axis		two axes
	one crisis		two crises
	one oasis		two oases
	one basis		two bases6

Words ending in *um* change to *a*.
Example:

We say			
	one memorandum	but	two memoranda
	one rostrum		two rostra

Words ending in *eau*, add *x*.
Example:

We say			
	one plateau	but	two plateaux
	one bureau		two bureaux

PRACTICE : FORMING THE PLURAL

Let us look at a few of these Rules at a time.

---

1. **To most words we simply add *s*.**
2. **To words ending in a *hissing s* add *es*.**
3. **Words ending in a *y* which is preceded by a consonant, change the *y* to an *i* and add *es*.**
4. **Words ending in a *y* which is preceded by a vowel, simply add *s*.**

Exercise Twelve: _____

Practising these four Rules only, write the *plural* of these words. In the brackets next to the word write 1, 2, 3 or 4 according to the Rule number above. The first three have been done for you.

donkey	__donkeys__ (_4_)	lamp	___lamps___ (_1_)	salary	__salaries__ (_3_)
dress	_____ (__)	baby	_____ (__)	lady	_____ (__)
book	_____ (__)	stage	_____ (__)	fox	_____ (__)
holiday	_____ (__)	toy	_____ (__)	canary	_____ (__)
village	_____ (__)	church	_____ (__)	lamp	_____ (__)
injury	_____ (__)	garden	_____ (__)	difficulty	_____ (__)
witch	_____ (__)	runway	_____ (__)	address	_____ (__)
chimney	_____ (__)	success	_____ (__)	jockey	_____ (__)
library	_____ (__)	mattress	_____ (__)	authority	_____ (__)
valley	_____ (__)	company	_____ (__)	journey	_____ (__)
curtain	_____ (__)	brooch	_____ (__)	chair	_____ (__)
stitch	_____ (__)	monkey	_____ (__)	daisy	_____ (__)

---

5. **Most words ending in *f* (or *fe*), change the *f* to a *v* and add *es*.**
6. **Some words ending in *f* simply add *s*.**
7. **Words ending in *o* or a vowel and *o*, add *es*.**
8. **Some words ending in *o*, simply add *s*.**
9. **Some words change completely.**
10. **Some words do not change at all.**

Exercise Thirteen: _____

Practising Rules 5 to 10 only, write the *plural* of these words. To help you, the number of the Rule which you should apply is given to you in the brackets next to the word. The first three have been done for you.

policeman	(9) _policemen_	wife	(5) __wives__	salmon	(10) __salmon__
piano	(8) _____	housewife	(5) _____	cliff	(6) _____
cargo	(7) _____	goose	(9) _____	half	(5) _____
tooth	(9) _____	elf	(5) _____	volcano	(7) _____
hero	(7) _____	cuff	(6) _____	cod	(10) _____
chief	(6) _____	wolf	(5) _____	ox	(9) _____
potato	(7) _____	solo	(8) _____	cello	(8) _____
sheep	(10) _____	child	(9) _____	roof	(6) _____
tomato	(7) _____	loaf	(5) _____	deer	(10) _____

> 11. **There is no singular form of some words.**
>   **They are always in the plural.**
> 12. **Some nouns have two plural forms.**

Exercise Fourteen: _____

Find three words of your own that have no singular form and are always in the plural.

_____

Find three words of your own that have two plural forms.

_____

> 13. **To words made up of more than one word,**
>   **add *s* to the main word.**
> 14. **Words ending in *us*, change to *i***
>
> | | |
> |---|---|
> | *is* | *es* |
> | *um* | *a* |
> | *eau* | *eaux* |

Exercise Fifteen: _____

Practising Rules 13 and 14 only, write the *plural* of these words. Put the number of the Rule you are applying in the brackets next to the word.

bureau	(__) _____	crisis	(__) _____
rostrum	(__) _____	bye-law	(__) _____
teaspoonful	(__) _____	oasis	(__) _____
centrum	(__) _____	brother-in-law	(__) _____
daughter-in-law	(__) _____	basis	(__) _____
radius	(__) _____	memorandum	(__) _____
passer-by	(__) _____	fungus	(__) _____
chateau	(__) _____	lady-in-waiting	(__) _____
mother-in-law	(__) _____	terminus	(__) _____
plateau	(__) _____	axis	(__) _____

Exercise Sixteen: _____

Referring to the 14 Rules for *forming the plural* of a word, write the *plural* of the following words on the line provided.

mouse	_____	turkey	_____
salmon	_____	shelf	_____
chief	_____	plateau	_____
potato	_____	passer-by	_____
wife	_____	terminus	_____
scratch	_____	latch	_____
spectacles	_____	ox	_____
hero	_____	life	_____
thief	_____	monkey	_____
daughter-in-law	_____	brooch	_____
diary	_____	table	_____

penny (2) _____   video _____

dish _____   valley _____

baby _____   wolf _____

railway _____   scissors _____

daisy _____   gas _____

chateau _____   man-of-war _____

banjo _____   radius _____

fungus _____   injury _____

leaf _____   cod _____

cuckoo _____   genius _____

torch _____   giraffe _____

memorandum _____   basis _____

volcano _____   trousers _____

tablespoonful _____   axis _____

Exercise Seventeen: _____

Write the *singular* form of the following words. Write in the brackets next to the word, the number of the Rule which has been applied in forming the plural (1 to 14).

chiefs (__) _____   plateaux (__) _____

cliffs (__) _____   ladies (__) _____

rostra (__) _____   valleys (__) _____

teeth (__) _____   splashes (__) _____

thieves (__) _____   injuries (__) _____

heroes (__) _____   monkeys (__) _____

fungi (__) _____   solos (__) _____

daisies (__) _____   memoranda (__) _____

cries (__) _____   bureaux (__) _____

crises	(___) _____	axes	(___) _____
policemen	(___) _____	passers-by	(___) _____
potatoes	(___) _____	spectacles	(___) _____
curtains	(___) _____	wives	(___) _____
termini	(___) _____	oxen	(___) _____
salaries	(___) _____	deer	(___) _____
mice	(___) _____	jockeys	(___) _____
couches	(___) _____	alloys	(___) _____
radii	(___) _____	brothers-in-law	(___) _____

Exercise Eighteen: _____

Choose the correct form of the *plural* from the alternatives given. Delete the incorrect spelling and then rewrite the correct spelling on the line provided.

valley	vallies	valleys	_____	goose	gooses	geese	_____
bureau	bureaus	bureaux	_____	thief	thieves	thiefs	_____
dish	dishs	dishes	_____	chief	chieves	chiefs	_____
shelf	shelves	shelfes	_____	roof	roofs	rooves	_____
passer-by	passers-by	passer-bys	_____	chimney	chimnies	chimneys	_____
potato	potatos	potatoes	_____	library	librarys	libraries	_____
diary	diaries	diarys	_____	basis	bases	basises	_____
mouse	mouses	mice	_____	wife	wives	wifes	_____
monkey	monkeys	monkies	_____	salary	salaries	salarys	_____

s OR *es* ON THE END OF A WORD

> **1. *s* or *es* on the end of a word makes a word plural.**
> **2. *s* is also added to a verb in the third person singular, that is after he, she, it, one, or the name of a person or thing.**

Example:

John *HITS* the ball.

The cat *DRINKS* its milk.

One SINGS like this.

He *RUNS* quickly.

She *LOVES* her kitten.

Exercise Nineteen: _____

Put *s* where you need one on the verbs below.

he kick	I run
they skip	she read
Robert run	Jackie play
James bang the drum with his fist.	Hayley sing a song in the choir.
They clap their hands to the rythmn.	Brian drive his car fast.

The verb (or doing word) always agrees with the *subject* of the verb, that is, the person or thing doing the action of the verb.
Example:

The boy *kicks* the ball.

The verb (or action word) is *kicks*.
The thing or person doing the kicking is the boy.

boy therefore, is the *subject* of the *verb*.

Boy is singular. The correct (singular) form of the verb then is *kicks* (singular).

When the subject of the verb is in the plural, the verb must agree with it, that is, also be in the plural. Hence we say:

The boys *are playing* football.

Is playing is in the singular. Only one boy *is playing*, boys *are playing*.

Be aware that sometimes it is necessary to change other words in a sentence to agree with the subject after it has been put into the plural.

Exercise Twenty: _____

Rewrite these sentences changing everything from the singular into the plural. Make as many changes as are necessary.

1. The book of the child is on the shelf.

   _____

2. The policeman was stopped by the passer-by just as the thief was stealing the purse from his mother-in-law.

   _____

   _____

3. The football player sustained an injury to his foot which prevented him from playing in the match.

_____

_____

4. The wife of the chief is wearing a dress with pink spots on it.

_____

_____

5. On the table there was a knife and fork, a potato, a tomato and a loaf on a dish.

_____

_____

6. At the concert the lady sang a solo to the cello, a solo to the piano and one to the banjo.

_____

_____

_____

7. At the zoo I saw a mouse, a deer, a turkey, a fox, a wolf, a kangaroo, an ostrich, a monkey, a hippopotamus, an ass and a horse with his hoof covered in fungus.

_____

_____

_____

8. He received a memorandum from the bureau asking him to avert the crisis which might occur if he did not ask his secretary for the key to the studio.

_____

_____

_____

_____

THE APOSTROPHE

An apostrophe is a small raised comma which has two functions.

> **A. An apostrophe is used to *show the ownership* of something.**
> **B. In a contraction, an apostophe *takes the place of a missing letter or letters*.**

A. To Show *Ownership*

When an apostophe is used to show the *ownership* of something it takes the place of the word *of*. The small raised comma either precedes an *s* or comes after an *s* which is added to the end of a word.
Example:

the football of my brother

This could be written:

my brother's football

Example:

the books of the girls

could be rewritten:

the girls' books

In both cases:
The apostrophe goes before or after the letter *s*.

A word ends in '*s* or *s*' to show that it is the owner of whatever immediately follows it.

---

1. To decide whether the apostrophe goes before or after the *s* you must ask the question:
WHO IS THE OWNER?
2. The apostrophe is placed immediately after the answer.

Example:
WHO IS THE OWNER here?

the dog of the lady
Answer: the lady   (singular noun)

Place the apostrophe immediately after the answer.

the lady's dog
Here, the noun *lady* is singular.
In this case the apostrophe precedes the '*s*.

WHO IS THE OWNER here?

the books of the boys
Answer: the boys   (plural noun)

Place the apostrophe immediately after the answer.

the boys' books
Here, the noun *boys* is plural.
In this case the apostrophe goes after the *s*'.

NOTE:

1. If the owner's name (singular or plural) already ends in *s*, there is no need to add another *s*. Simply add the apostrophe.

Example:

the bicycle of Mr Jones (singular)

becomes:

Mr Jones' bicycle
(This would be pronounced Mr Jonses bicycle)

Example:

the rattles of the babies (plural)

becomes:

the babies' rattles

2. If the noun changes completely in the plural (in accordance with Rule 9 of Forming the Plural) treat the noun as if it were in the singular and use 's.

Example:

the apples of the children

becomes:

the children's apples

If you always apply the two Rules:

1. Ask : *WHO IS THE OWNER?*
2. Place the apostrophe immediately after the answer,

there should never be a problem.

Exercise Twenty-One:_____

Rewrite each phrase on the line provided replacing the word *of* with an *apostrophe*.
Remember ask : WHO IS THE OWNER?
                        Place the apostrophe immediately after the answer.

the book of the boy   _____

the dolls of the girls   _____

the hats of the lady   _____

the bag of the old man   _____

the crying of the baby   _____

the trunk of the elephant   _____

the home of the dogs   _____

the dolls of the girl _____

the wings of the butterflies _____

the crying of the babies _____

the bicycle of Mr. Jones _____

the toys of the children _____

the hat of Mrs. Williams _____

the wheels of the bus _____

the book of the teacher _____

the raging of the seas _____

the scooter of Peter _____

the bonnet of the car _____

the food of the oxen _____

the roar of the traffic _____

Exercise Twenty-Two: _____

Rewrite the following phrases in two ways. Firstly, reword using the word *of*. Secondly, rewrite placing the *apostrophe* correctly.

Example:
    would be reworded:
    and rewritten:

the boys bicycle
the bicycle of the boy
the boy's bicycle

Mr. Jones van _____ _____

the childrens footballs _____ _____

the ladies scarves _____ _____

the babys rattle _____ _____

the babies toys _____ _____

the churches towers _____ _____

the deers antlers _____ _____

the Eskimos home _____ _____

the horses tail _____ _____

the horses tails   _____   _____

the dogs growl   _____   _____

the ladies shoes   _____   _____

the soldiers injury   _____   _____

the cars engine   _____   _____

the cars engines   _____   _____

the ladies shouts   _____   _____

the childrens voices   _____   _____

the tomatoes skins   _____   _____

the tomatos skin   _____   _____

the workmens tools   _____   _____

Exercise Twenty-Three:_____

Read these sentences carefully then rewrite adding an *apostrophe* where necessary. Be careful, some of the sentences may not need an apostrophe at all!

1. My sisters friend wears pink trousers.

   _____

2. The cat heard the mices squeaks and went to investigate.

   _____

3. People who live in glass houses should not throw stones.

   _____

4. The children listened to Mr. Jones words in amazement.

   _____

5. I bought that rack of spices some weeks ago.

   _____

6. The cows tail swished from side to side to flick away the flies.

   _____

7. Mother was cross because the childrens clothes had not been put away.

   _____

8. The athletes arms were tense as he waited for the crack of the starting pistol.

   _____

9. Despite the pilots efforts, the aeroplane skidded as the wheels touched the runway.

   _____

10. We spent two weeks holiday at the seaside.

   _____

Exercise Twenty-Four: _____

Following the instructions, write a phrase of three words taking care to place the *apostrophe* in the correct place each time.

Example: more than one book of more than one child
becomes: the children's books

more than one hat of one lady_____

more than one bag of more than one student _____

one bicycle of one toddler _____

one garden of one house _____

more than one tooth of more than one child _____

more than one mouse of more than one mouse_____

one mouse of one mouse _____

more than one cub of more than one fox _____

one cub of one fox_____

more than one box of more than one child_____

B. An Apostrophe used in *Contraction*

When we talk, we often run two words together, missing out one or more letters. This short way of writing words is called a *contraction*.

In a contraction an apostrophe is used where the letters are missing.

Example:

| | is not | can be shortened to | isn't |
| | did not | | didn't |

In both cases the two words are joined together, and an *apostrophe* takes the place of the letter *o* which is omitted.

Exercise Twenty-Five: _____

Rewrite the following pairs of words in shortened form, using an *apostrophe* in place of the letter or letters omitted.

A. *not* can be shortened to *n't*
do not   _____don't_____   need not   _____

did not   _____   cannot   _____

are not   _____   will not   _____

must not   _____   shall not   _____

were not   _____   was not   _____

could not   _____   has not   _____

should not   _____   have not   _____

would not   _____   had not   _____

might not   _____   does not   _____

B. *is* and *has* can both be shortened to *'s*
he is   _____he's_____   she is   _____

it is   _____   here is   _____

who is?   _____   there is   _____

what is?   _____   where is?   _____

how is?   _____   that is   _____

he has   _____   he is   _____

she has   _____   it has   _____

C. *have* can be shortened to *'ve*
I have   _____I've_____   we have   _____

you have   _____   they have   _____

D. *are* can be shortened to *'re*
you are   _____you're_____

we are   _____   they are   _____

E. *would* can be shortened to *'d*
I would   _____I'd_____

you would   _____   I would   _____

he would   _____   they would   _____

she would   _____   who would?   _____

we would   _____   there would   _____

F. *will* can be shortened to '*ll*

I will	_____I'll_____	you will	_____
he will	_____	they will	_____
she will	_____	who will?	_____
it will	_____	there will	_____
we will	_____	that will	_____

Exercise Twenty-Six: _____

Put an *apostrophe* in these words where a letter (or letters) has been left out, then write out the long form alongside the *contraction*.

c a n t	_____	s h e s	_____	y o u r e	_____
h e l l	_____	I l l	_____	I m	_____
t h e y r e	_____	w h e r e s	_____	h a d n t	_____
y o u l l	_____	s h e d	_____	t h a t s	_____
d o n t	_____	y o u d	_____	w a s n t	_____
i t s	_____	t h e y v e	_____	I d	_____
s h e l l	_____	w e l l	_____	d o e s n t	_____
t h e r e s	_____	h a s n t	_____	i s n t	_____
h o w s ?	_____	w h o s ?	_____	w e v e	_____

Exercise Twenty-Seven: _____

Rewrite each of these sentences using *contractions* in place of the words in italics.

She would like to come if *you would* let her.

_____

I will go to the beach if *it is* a sunny day.

_____

Do not let me delay you - *I will* catch you up later.

_____

It is certain *they are* going to win.

_____

There will be no more pocket money until *you are* good.

_____

When *you have* tidied your bedroom *we will* go.

_____

What is wrong? *Do not* worry, *you will* be alright.

_____

Where is the kitten? *I will* give it some milk.

_____

How is your knee? *He will* bandage it if *you will* let him.

_____

I will not leave until *you are* ready.

_____

Who is that person? *She is* very pretty!

_____

I have an idea which you *might not* like!

_____

Exercise Twenty-Eight: _____

Which letters have been left out of these sentences? Write out in full the word which has the *apostrophe*.

You're here at last!	_____	I haven't any money.	_____
They've been waiting for you.	_____	There's something over there!	_____
Now I'm ready.	_____	Can't I come?	_____
We'll go.	_____	What'll you do now?	_____
You'll like this!	_____	Isn't it lovely!	_____
It's a surprise!	_____	Peter's coming too.	_____
Who'll come with me?	_____	He's afraid.	_____
There'll be plenty to eat.	_____	I've taken the book.	_____
You've left your coat.	_____	They'll be here soon.	_____
Aren't you coming?	_____	Don't be cruel!	_____

Exercise Twenty-Nine: _____

There are 54 deliberate mistakes connected with the presence or absence of *apostrophes* in the following sentences. Rewrite each sentence correcting the mistakes. Both functions of the *apostrophe* have been included. The number of mistakes in each sentence is shown in brackets.

1. Whos taken Roberts book out of his desk? Hes looked everywhere for it and hes had to borrow Louises. Now she want's it back. (6)

   _____

2. Whens lunch? Im starving! I promised to go to Christophers house and hell be waiting for me. Please hurry! (4)

   _____

3. The dogs feet had left a track of prints' across the soils smooth surface of the flower bed in the park. (3)

   _____

4. Emmas mother wasnt in. Shed left with the childrens grandparent's and wasnt due back until later. (6)

   _____

5. Michaels looking for Charles books. Hes found Williams but he cant find Charles. He thinks theyve been stolen, but hopes' hes wrong. (9)

   _____

6. James shoes are the same as Toms but different from Tims. Alex has the same shoes but theyre a different colour. (4)

   _____

   _____

7. The seas' are raging and the waves' are crashing against the cliffs face. Itll do a lot of damage to the birds nests there. Theyll tumble into the waters below and be lost on the cliffs rocks'. (8)

   _____

   _____

   _____

8. Whos coming to town with me? Ive to go soon so dont take too long to get ready. Well go in Brians car. Its fast and well get theyre quicker. (8)

   _____

   _____

   _____

9. Mines the one with bananas'. I dont like strawberry's so thatll be yours'. (6)

   _____

   _____

TRICKY WORDS

In this section I shall look at some of the most commonly used words which have more than one spelling (and meaning) and which often present difficulties.

To, Too and *Two*

> **To** is used:
> > to show movement towards something (a noun);
> > in front of a verb.

Example:

riding *to* town; cycling *to* the beach; walking *to* school.
to read a letter; *to* cycle to school; *to* write a story.

> **Too** means:
> > more than enough;
> > also, as well.

Example:

She is *too* fat. The hole is *too* small. He is *too* slow.
He is coming. She is coming *too*. I am tired. You are tired *too*.

> **Two** is a number.

Example:

Two and three equal five. *Two* and *two* equal four.

Exercise Thirty:_____

Use the correct form of *to, too* or *two*, in the spaces below.

1. He is coming _____ stay with us; she is coming _____.

2. It is _____ late _____ go _____ town. It is past _____o'clock.

3. That book was _____ expensive. I decided _____ buy this one instead.

4. I am going _____ read you _____ stories tonight.

5. _____ children will be chosen _____ fly _____ Florida for _____ weeks _____ stay in Disneyworld.

6. _____ o'clock is _____ soon _____ leave.

Their, There and *They're*

> ### *Their* means:
> belonging to them.

Example:

The girls lost *their* books. The boys forgot *their* kit.

> ### *There*:
> begins a sentence;
> shows a place.

Example:

There is going to be a party. *There* are many people there.
We shall go *there* later. Wait *there* and I shall come.

> ### *They're*:
> is a contraction for *they are*.

Example:

They're late. *They're* coming. *They're* here now.

Exercise Thirty-One: _____

Choose the correct *their, there* or *they're* to write into these sentences.

1. _____ is going to be trouble. The twins cannot find _____ books.

2. The boys must go to the theatre and wait for you _____. _____ should be plenty of tickets left. I hope _____ not late.

3. Will _____ be space for _____ sister?

4. After _____ victory, the team thanked _____ captain for all his hard work.

5. I saw the children over _____. _____ walking _____ dog.

6. _____ leaving us soon. _____ will be a farewell party to celebrate _____ success.

Where, were and *we're*

Where means:
> what place?

Example:
> *Where* are you going tonight? *Where* did you buy that book?

Were:
> is the plural form of *was*.

Example:
> The boy was coming. The boys *were* coming.

We're:
> is a contraction for *we are*.

Example:
> *We're* going now. *We're* taking the bus.

Exercise Thirty-Two: _____

Choose the correct spelling of *where, were* or *we're* to complete the following sentences.

1. _____ are you going tonight? _____ hoping we can join you.

2. There _____ many children in the park. _____ _____ their mothers?

3. Children _____ playing in the street _____ cars _____ parked last week.

4. Mother wondered _____ her children _____.

5. _____ is the jumper we gave you? _____ delighted it fits.

6. _____ going on holiday today. _____ are you going? _____ going to America.

Hear and *Here*

You *hear* with your ears.

Example:
> I *hear* the television but I can't see it.

> **Here** means:
> in this place.

Example:

I left the book *here*. *Here* is the book you are looking for.

Exercise Thirty-Three: _____

Write *here* or *hear* in the spaces below.

1. _____ is the telephone. I hope you can _____ her voice.

2. Wait _____ until I have finished.

3. _____ me and _____ me well! You will wait _____ until the bus arrives!

4. Did you _____ that noise? I think it came from in _____.

5. _____ is the watch. Place it to you ear. Can you _____ the faint ticking?

6. _____ Peter! Come and get your lunch _____.

Its and *It's*

> *It* is a pronoun. When something belongs to *it* we say **its**
> (a possessive pronoun). <u>There is no apostrophe.</u>

Example:

The cat is drinking *its* milk. The puppy wagged *its* tail.

> **It's** is a contraction of *it is*.

Example:

It's getting late. *It's* time to go home.

Exercise Thirty-Four: _____

Complete the following sentences inserting the correct form of *its* or *it's*.

1. Do you think _____ going to rain today?

2. The tent is loosing _____ colour in the sun. _____ a shame! It used to be bright orange!

3. The cat caught a shrew in _____ claws.

4. _____ Saturday! _____ today we are having a barbeque!

5. My potted plant is loosing all of _____ leaves. _____ too dry.

6. _____ late, and the dog is pulling _____ lead. I must go!

Your and *You're*

Your means: belonging to you.

Example:

    It's *your* bat and *your* ball but I would like to play.

You're is a contraction of *you are*.

Example:

    You're getting tall. I think *you're* very handsome.

Exercise Thirty-Five:_____

Use the correct *your* or *you're* in the spaces below.

1. If _____ late, ask _____ friend to help you.

2. Have you had _____ lunch yet? I should think _____ hungry.

3. I hope _____ happy with _____ christmas present.

4. I think _____ the luckiest person in _____ class.

5. Do you usually eat _____ crisps with _____ gloves on?

6. _____ certain to find _____ way if you follow the path.

R U L E   S U M M A R I E S

Here you are asked to do three things:
1. Read through all the Rules that have been identified in this book, one at a time.
2. When you are ready, fill in all the missing words in the Rule Summaries below.
3. Explain in your own words what is meant by each Rule, making reference to the examples given.

Read through all the Rules concerning *e* **AT THE END OF A WORD** on pages 1 to 3. When you are ready, complete the following Rule Summary without referring to that section.

The *e* at the end of a word says nothing at all but has _____ important jobs to do.
1. To make a _____ say its *name*.
2. To follow ___ because no English word ends in ___ alone.
3. To make ___ say___.
4. To make ___ say ___.
5. To '_____ ____' an ___ if you cannot take it off and be left with a _____ _____.

Now turn back to page 3 and check your answer.

KEEPING YOUR OWN RECORD OF THE SPELLING RULES IN THESE BOOKS

To keep a permanent record of the Spelling Rules in these books - a record to which you can refer at any time - you need a pack of 5ins x 8ins index cards and an index card box or A5 file. You have already made Twenty-One Record Cards from Books One and Two. Continue here with Card Twenty-Two.

CARD TWENTY-TWO:
Once you have corrected the Rule Summary concerning *e* **AT THE END OF A WORD,** carefully copy these Rules from page 3 onto the first side of Card Twenty-Two.

On the reverse side of Card Twenty-Two put the heading *e* **AT THE END OF A WORD** and in your own words write about the importance of an *e* in the English language and how it has influenced the spelling and pronunciation of the spoken word.

CARD TWENTY-THREE:
Read about **THE *v* RULES** on pages 5 and 6. When you are ready, complete the following Rule Summary without referring to that section.

There are _____ Rules concerning **THE *v* SPELLING**.
1. Never end a word in *v* alone, always end _____.
2. Never use ____. Only ever use a single ___.
3. Never use ____. ___ before *v* says ___ so use _____ to say___.

Besides using *u* to say *u*, other letters which say *u* include:
1. ___ before *th*.
2. ___ before ___ and ___ can say *u*.

Turn back to page 6 to check your answers, then copy these Rules neatly onto the first side of Card Twenty-Three.

On the reverse of Card Twenty-Three list examples to illustrate each part of these Rules.

CARD TWENTY-FOUR:
Read through the notes about *s* **AT THE END OF A WORD** on pages 7 and 8 and when you are ready complete the following Rule Summary without referring to that section.

There are _____ ways of creating a *hissing s* sound at the end of a word:
___, ____, _____ and _____.

1. Use a single *s* if _____
   _____ .

2. Use *ss* after a _____ vowel in accordance with the ____ Rule.
3. Use ___ or ___ after a _____ vowel or a _____ vowel and a consonant. ____ is more usual, so when in doubt, use____.

Check your answers by referring to page 8. Once you have corrected the Rule Summary above, copy it carefully and neatly onto the first side of Card Twenty-Four.

On the reverse side of Card Twenty-Four:
a. Discuss these Rules highlighting your explanation with many Examples.
b. Record the *se* endings which are listed on page 8.
c. With reference to the functions of a silent *e*, explain when an *s* can and cannot be taken off a word.

CARD TWENTY-FIVE:
Read the notes on **SPELLING THE *z* SOUND** on pages 11 to 13 and then complete the following Rule Summary without referring to that section.

There are _____ ways to spell the *z* sound:
1. An *s* is usually pronounced ___, but occasionally has a ___ sound.
(*ss* in the middle of a word is often pronounced *z*.)
2. Use ___ for a ___ sound at the beginning of a word, never___.
3. In the middle of a word use ___, ____, ___ or ____ for a *z* sound. ___ is the most common.
4. Use ____ only for the *z* sound at the end of a word after a _____ vowel, never___.
5. Use ____ or ____ at the end of a word after a _____ vowel sound which follows either the pattern: Vowel - consonant - *silent e*, or a vowel _____.
___ is more common.

Read pages 11 to 13 to check your answers. Then copy the above Rule onto the first side of Card Twenty-Five.

On the reverse of Card Twenty-Five:
a. List three Examples to illustrate each part of the Rule.
b. Compare the sounds of words ending in *ss* and *zz*, giving Examples.
c. Make a note of any *exceptions* to these Rules.

CARDS TWENTY-SIX, TWENTY-SEVEN and TWENTY-EIGHT:
FORMING THE PLURAL
Read through the fourteen rules for **FORMING THE PLURAL** on pages 14 to 19. Then, without referring to those notes, complete the following:

We say that something is in the *SINGULAR* when we are talking about ____ noun.

We say that a noun is in the *PLURAL* when we are talking about _____.
There are ____ Rules for forming the plural of a noun.

1. The most usual ending when forming the plural is to add ___.
2. For words ending in a hissing sound, such as ____, ____, ___, ___ and ____,
   add____.
3. Words ending in *y* which is immediately _____ by a consonant, change the
   ___ to an ___ and add _____.
4. If there is a vowel immediately preceding the *y*, we just ____ ___.
5. Most words ending in *f,* change the ___ to a ___ and add _____.
6. Some words ending in *f* simply add ___.
7. Words ending in *o,* or a _____ plus *o,* add ____.
8. Some words ending in *o,* especially words associated with _____, add ___.
9. Some words change _____.
10. Some words do not _____ at all.
11. Some words are always in the _____.
12. Some nouns have ____ _____ forms.
13. Add the *s* to the _____ word when the noun is made up of more than one word
    (often _____).
14. Change *us* to ___, *is* to _____, *um* to ___ and to words ending in *eau,* add ___.

Check these answers by referring to pages 14 to 19, and then copy these Rules, putting in your own
Examples as you do so, onto Cards Twenty-Six and Twenty-Seven.

On the first side of Card Twenty-Eight, copy these words and alongside write the plural of each. Put the
number of the Rule, as above, in brackets next to each word. The first one has been completed for you.

donkey	____donkeys____	(_4_)	difficulty	_____	(__)	church	_____	(__)
lamp	_____	(__)	calf	_____	(__)	piano	_____	(__)
basis	_____	(__)	plateau	_____	(__)	son-in-law	_____	(__)
baby	_____	(__)	tooth	_____	(__)	torch	_____	(__)
fungus	_____	(__)	rostrum	_____	(__)	passer-by	_____	(__)
sheep	_____	(__)	scissors	_____	(__)	chief	_____	(__)
thief	_____	(__)	toy	_____	(__)	tomato	_____	(__)

On the reverse side of Card Twenty-Eight, alongside the number of the Rule, list all the Examples of
Rules 5, 6, 7, 8, 9 and 10 as indicated under each separate Rule, on pages 15 to 16.
Answers: 1, 14, 3, 14, 10, 5, 3, 5, 14, 9, 14, 11, 4, 2, 7, 13, 2, 13, 8, 7.

CARD TWENTY-NINE:
Read the notes about *s* OR *es* ON THE END OF A WORD on page 22 and when you are ready,
complete the following Rule Summary without referring to that section:

1. ___ or _____ on the end of a word makes a word _____.
2. ___ is also added to a _____ in the _____ person _____, that is after ____,
   _____, ____, _____ or the name of the _____ or _____.

Check your answer by referring to page 22.

Onto the first side of Card Twenty-Nine, copy carefully and neatly the Rule above.

On the reverse side of Card Twenty-Nine make your own notes explaining what is meant by the **SUBJECT** of a verb and the **AGREEMENT** of a subject with the verb.

CARD THIRTY and THIRTY-ONE:
Read all the notes about an **APOSTROPHE** on pages 24 to 29 and when you are ready complete the following Rule Summary without reference to that section.

1. An apostrophe is a small raised _____.
   It has _____ functions:
a. An apostophe is used to _____ ____ _____ of something.
b. In a _____ an apostrophe takes the place of a _____ _____
   or letters.

A. TO SHOW OWNERSHIP
To decide whether an apostrophe goes _____ or _____ the letter ___ ask the question:

_____

The apostrophe is placed _____ _____ the answer.

B. IN A CONTRACTION
When we talk, we often run two words together, missing out one or more _____.
This short way of writing words is called a _____. An apostrophe takes the place of the _____ or _____ which are missing.

Check your answers by referring to pages 24, 25 and 29.

Copy these notes carefully and accurately onto Card Thirty.

On the first side of Card Thirty-One discuss the two uses of the apostophe, using examples from the text to help you fully explain these two uses.
Mention in particular the position of an apostrophe:
a. When the owner's name ends in *s*, and
b. When a noun *changes completely* in the plural, for example *child* to *children*.

CARD THIRTY-TWO:
Read the notes on pages 34 to 38 regarding **TRICKY WORDS** and when you are ready complete the following Rule Summaries without referring to those pages.

To is used _____and _____
Too means_____and _____
Two is _____
Their means_____
There begins_____and _____
They're is_____
Where means _____
Were is_____
We're is _____
You *hear* _____
Here means _____

Its is a _____ There is no _____

It's is _____

Your means _____

You're is _____

Turn back to pages 34 to 38 to check your answers, then copy the above notes onto the first side of Card Thirty-Two.

On the reverse side of Card Thirty-Two make any notes that will help you to better remember these *Tricky Words*.

CARD THIRTY-THREE:

Make a note of any of the words in Book Three which you have found difficult to remember and which you need to look at again. Alongside each word make a note of the Rule to which it belongs and a page reference, so you can look it up and read over the Rule again. Try to learn these words.

Words I have found difficult to remember in Book Three which I need to look at again:

WORD	RULE	PAGE	LEARNT

ANSWERS

Working *down* the Exercises, the Answers are as follows:

Exercise 1

5	5
3	1 and 5
3	√
2	1
3	1 and 4
1	1 and 5
1 and 4	2
1 and 5	√
5	4
3	√
2	3
2	1
3	√
2	3
3	1 and 5
1	√
2	3
1	√
2	5
3	3
1	√
1 and 5	3
1	4
3	4
1	1 and 5
3	3
3	1 and 4
3	1 and 4
1 and 4	1
3	1 and 5
3	1 and 2
2	2
3	2
1 and 4	2
3	1
1 and 5	4
2	1 and 5
1	1

Exercise 2

horse, √, else, house, nurse, cover, discover, survive, goose, curse, detective, love, hover, heave, dose, √, choose, cause, suppose, √, worse, chase, close, case

oven, observe, extravagant, glove, deserve, cover, discover, survive, goose, curse, detective, love, hover, heave, dose, √, choose, cause, suppose, √, worse, chase, close, case

nothing, among, shovel, wonder, shutter, front, farce, kiss, lasts, fence, noose, boss, empress, sings, moss

place, falls, else, lasts, bus, crease, nonsense, loose, noise, purse, business

√, nurse, mouse, because, zero, recognise or ze, √, dizzy, noise, dissolve, business, prize, president, zip, choose

fizz, breeze

Exercise 3

recover, nerve, lover, gave, vulgar, monkey, another, justice, spice, sparse, gas, come, upper, love, brother, prince, loss, bubble, nonsense, cover, above, arrive, curve, smother, discover, mother

Exercise 4

honey, month, cause, suppose, √, above, cover, bubble, nonsense, brother, prince, loss, love, upper, come, educate, glove, London, perceive, purple, muscle, comfort, buttercup

Exercise 8

congress, purse, month, sense, fudge, above, confess, cover, bubble, nonsense, brother, prince, loss, house, puzzle, disease, amuse, reduce, moss, disease

kiss, lasts, fence, noose, boss, false, grease, choose

Exercise 9

sense, √, horse, √, house, else, loss, √, goose, √, base, spice, recess, dance, rinse, pulse, cross, horse, cause, scissors

nonsense, loose, purse, noose, false, grease, moss, disease

Exercise 10

graze, reason, freeze, possess

Exercise 11

1. puzzle because
   zinc dissolve
2. result disease dozen
   zoo recognised or ized
3. pleased prize
   graze noise
4. whose cousin visit
   president reasonable monkeys
5. freezes zero
6. rose horizon
7. please choose
   dazzled dizzy
8. amuse these
   because easier
   scissors razor
   transistor

Exercise 12

dresses 2
books 1
holidays 4
villages 1
injuries 3
witches 2
chimneys 4
libraries 3
valleys 4
curtains 1
stitches 2
babies 3
stages 1
toys 4
churches 2
gardens 1
runways 4
successes 2
mattresses 2
companies 3
brooches 2
monkeys 4
ladies 3
foxes 2
canaries 3
lamps 1
difficulties 3
addresses 2
jockeys 4
authorities 3
journeys 4

chairs 1
daisies 3

Exercise 13

pianos	chateaux 14	memoranda
cargoes	mothers-in-law 13	volcanoes or volcanos
teeth	plateaux 14	tablespoonsful
heroes	crises 14	turkeys
chiefs	bye-laws 13	shelves
potatoes	oases 14	plateaux
sheep	brothers-in-law 13	passers-by
tomatoes	bases 14	termini
housewives	memoranda 14	latches
geese	fungi 14	oxen
elves	ladies-in-waiting 13	lives
cuffs	termini 14	monkeys
wolves	axes 14	brooches
solos		
children		
loaves		
cliffs		
halves		
volcanoes		
cod		
oxen		
cellos		
roofs		
deer		

Exercise 16

mice	daisy 3
salmon	cry 3
chiefs	crisis 14
potatoes	policeman 9
wives	potato 7
scratches	curtain 1
spectacles	terminus 14
heroes	salary 3
thieves	mouse 9
daughters-in-law	couch 2
diaries	radius 14
pennies and pence	plateau 14
dishes	lady 3
babies	

Exercise 19

kicks	tables
skip	videos
runs	valleys
bangs	wolves
clap	scissors
run	gases
reads	men of war
plays	radii
sings	injuries
drives	cod
	genii (or geniuses)
	giraffes
	bases
	trousers
	axes

valley 4	diaries
splash 2	mice
injury 3	monkeys
monkey 4	geese
solo 8	thieves
memorandum 14	chiefs
bureau 14	roofs
axis 14	chimneys
passer-by 13	libraries
spectacles 11	bases
wife 5	wives
ox 9	salaries
deer 10	
jockey 4	
alloy 4	
brother-in-law 13	

Exercise 17

chief 6	
cliff 1 or 6	
rostrum 14	
tooth 9	
thief 5	
hero 7	
fungus 14	

Exercise 18

valleys
bureaux
dishes
shelves
passers-by
potatoes

Exercise 15

bureaux 14
rostra 14
teaspoonsful 13
centra 14
daughters-in-law 13
radii 14
passers-by 13

Exercise 20

1. The books of the children are on the shelves.
2. The policemen were stopped by the passers-by just as the thieves were stealing the purses from their mothers-in-law.
3. The football players sustained injuries to their feet which prevented them from playing in the matches.
4. The wives of the chiefs are wearing dresses with pink spots on them.
5. On the tables there were some knives and forks, some potatoes, some tomatoes and some loaves on some dishes.
6. At the concerts the ladies sang some solos to the cellos, some solos to the pianos and some to the banjos (or banjoes).
7. At the zoos we saw some mice, some deer, some turkeys, some foxes, some wolves, some kangaroos, some ostriches, some monkeys, some hippopotami (or hippopotamuses), some asses and some horses with their hoofs (or hooves) covered in fungi.
8. They received some memoranda from the bureaux asking them to avert the crises which might occur if they did not ask their secretaries for the keys to the studios.

Exercise 21

the boy's book
the girls' dolls
the lady's hats
the old man's bag
the baby's crying
the elephant's trunk
the dogs' home
the girl's dolls
the butterflies' wings
the babies' crying
Mr. Jones' bicycle
the children's toys
Mrs. Williams' hat
the bus' wheels
the teacher's book
the seas' raging
Peter's scooter

Exercise 21 cont'd

the car's bonnet
the oxen's food
the traffic's roar

Exercise 22

the van of Mr. Jones; Mr. Jones' van
the footballs of the children; the children's footballs
the scarves of the ladies; the ladies' scarves
the rattle of the baby; the baby's rattle
the toys of the babies; the babies' toys
the towers of the churches; the churches' towers
the antlers of the deer; the deer's antlers
the home of the Eskimo; the Eskimo's home
the tail of the horse; the horse's tail
the tails of the horses; the horses' tails
the growl of the dog; the dog's growl
the shoes of the ladies; the ladies' shoes
the injury of the soldier; the soldier's injury
the engine of the car; the car's engine
the engines of the cars; the cars' engine.
the shouts of the ladies; the ladies' shouts

the voices of the children: the children's voices
the skins of the tomatoes; the tomatoes' skins
the skin of the tomato; the tomato's skin
the tools of the workmen; the workmen's tools

Exercise 23

1. My sister's friend wears pink trousers.
2. The cat heard the mice's squeaks and went to investigate.
3. No change.
4. The children listened to Mr. Jones' words in amazement.
5. No change.
6. The cow's tail swished from side to side to flick away the flies.
7. Mother was cross because the children's clothes had not been put away.
8. The athlete's arms were tense as he waited for the crack of the starting pistol.
9. Despite the pilot's efforts, the aeroplane skidded as the wheels touched the runway.
10. We spent two weeks' holiday at the seaside.

Exercise 24

the lady's hats
the students' bags
the toddler's bicycle
the house's garden
the children's teeth
the mouse's mouse
the foxes' cubs
the fox's cub
the children's boxes

Exercise 25

didn't
aren't
mustn't
weren't
couldn't
shouldn't
wouldn't
mightn't
needn't
can't
won't
shan't
wasn't
hasn't
haven't

hadn't	
doesn't	
it's	
who's?	
what's?	
how's?	
she's	
that's	
he's	
it's	
you've	
we've	
they've	
we're	
they're	
you'd	
she'd	
we'd	
I'd	
they'd	
who'd?	
there'd	
he'll	
she'll	
it'll	
we'll	
you'll	
they'll	
there'll	
who'll?	
they'll	
there'll	
that'll	

there's
where's?
I'll I will
you will
it is
she'd she would
you'd you would
they've they have
we'll we will
are not
have not
there is
can not
what will
is not
hadn't had not
that's that is
wasn't was not
I'd I would
doesn't does not
isn't is not
we've we have

how's?
she's she is
where's? where is?
who's? who is?
hasn't has not
you're you are
I'm I am
Peter is
he is

Exercise 26

can't cannot
he'll he will
who's she's
I'll you're
you'll you will
don't do not
where's I'll
how's he'll you'll

Exercise 27

she'd you'd
I'll it's
don't I'll
it's they're
there'll you're
you've we'll
what's don't you'll

Exercise 28

you are
they have
I am
we will
you will
it is
who will
there will
you have
are not

Exercise 29

1. who's Robert's he's he's Louise's wants
2. when's I'm Christopher's he'll
3. dog's (or dogs') prints soil's
4. Emma's wasn't she'd children's grandparents wasn't
5. Michael's Charles' he's William's can't Charles' they've hopes he's
6. James' Tom's Tim's they're
7. seas waves cliffs it'll birds' they'll cliffs (or cliffs')rocks
8. who's I've don't we'll Brian's it's we'll there
9. mine's bananas don't strawberries that'll yours

Exercise 30

1. to too
2. too to to two
3. too to
4. to two
5. two to to two to
6. Two too to

Exercise 31

1. There their
2. there There they're
3. there their
4. their their
5. there They're their
6. They're There their

Exercise 32

1. Where we're
2. were where we're
3. were where were
4. where were
5. Where Where We're
6. We're Where We're

Exercise 33

1. Here hear
2. here
3. Hear hear here
4. hear here
5. Here hear
6. Here here

Exercise 34

1. it's
2. its it's
3. its
4. it's it's
5. its it's
6. it's its

Exercise 35

1. you're your
2. your you're
3. you're your
4. you're your
5. your your
6. You're your